CRICKET

ANDY SELLINS

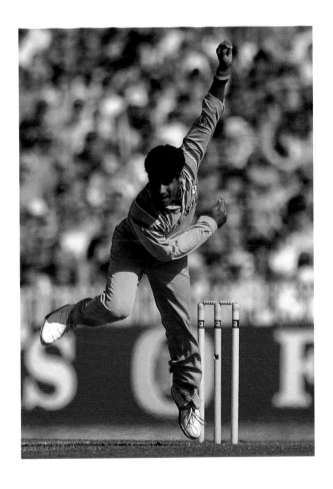

Wayland

Go For Sport!
Basketball
Cricket
Fishing
Gymnastics
Judo
Karate
Rugby
Soccer

Cover: Richie Richardson, one of the world's leading batsmen.

Acknowledgements
The publisher would like to thank Allsport for providing all the photographs used in this book. The artwork on pages 10, 17, 19, 23, 24 and 25 is by Malcolm Walker. The artwork on pages 11, 36, 37, 39 and 41 is by Jo Dennis (Indent).
The author would like to thank his father Dave Sellins for his technical advice and also his mother Eileen and Bev for all their support.

Series Editor: James Kerr
Designer: Malcolm Walker

First published in 1994 by
Wayland (Publishers) Limited,
61 Western Road,
Hove, East Sussex, BN3 1JD

British Library Cataloguing in Publication Data
Sellins, Andy
  Cricket - (Go for Sport! Series)
  I. Title II. Series
  796.358

ISBN 0-7502-1032-X

Typeset by Kudos Editorial and Design Services
Printed and bound in Italy by G.Canale and C.S.p.A.

Contents

INTRODUCTION 4

HISTORY AND DEVELOPMENT....6

ABOUT THE GAME 10

BATTING SKILLS 12

BOWLING SKILLS 21

WICKETKEEPING 26

FIELDING SKILLS 29

CAPTAINCY 32

FITNESS TRAINING....................35

SKILL TRAINING 39

EQUIPMENT 43

GLOSSARY 46

FURTHER READING AND

    INFORMATION 47

INDEX 48

INTRODUCTION

H itting the ball out of the ground, shattering a batsman's stumps or diving to take a one-handed catch – these are all part of the thrill of cricket. It's a team sport in which, while batting, you and your partner try to outplay the eleven players gathered around you.

Cricket is played in many parts of the world – on beaches, in parks, in the street and of course on all sorts of different cricket grounds. It is above all a sociable game. Winning is great, but losing with a smile on your face and making new friends is just as important.

You don't have to be highly talented to play cricket. In every country in which cricket is played, there are teams catering for the beginner right up to the professional player. One thing that players at every level find is that you can always improve your game, and your enjoyment of it, with practice. This book should help you to do just that.

Be warned though: once you get started you'll probably get hooked. You'll want to play more, read more and watch more cricket. You'll then find, like millions of cricket fans around the world, that there is so much to know about cricket that you will never really know it all.

Viv Richards – the greatest batsman ever?

▶ ▶ ▶ ▶

What a great place to play. This is the St.Kitts test match ground in the West Indies.

HISTORY AND DEVELOPMENT

Cricket played to current rules dates from the early eighteenth century in England. The first records come from the club at Hambledon, who were the strongest team in England. At this time most of the great elevens were run by noblemen, who bet heavily on the result of games.

In about 1800 the game took a strong hold in London, and Lord's cricket ground became the headquarters of cricket and the property of the Marylebone Cricket Club, better known as the MCC. In 1836 pads and gloves for batting and wicketkeeping were first used, and in 1864 – after much argument – overarm bowling was allowed.

During the second half of the nineteenth century, cricket developed rapidly in England and elsewhere. It was first played in the West Indies in the 1850s and in India in the 1820s. The game quickly caught on in Australia, with the earliest game played in 1803. By 1877 cricket had developed so quickly in Australia that in the first ever test match they defeated England in Melbourne.

In 1882 Australia beat England again at the Oval in London, even

Controversy and debate have always surrounded cricket, and never was this truer than in the 1932 'bodyline' series of test matches between Australia and England. The English bowlers deliberately bowled fast, short-pitched deliveries – called 'bouncers' – at the Australian batsmen's heads, making them give catches to the surrounding fielders. This almost led to an international incident, and the MCC had to change the laws, making such tactics illegal.

The 1990s have seen the controversy continue, with new laws allowing only two bouncers to be bowled in any one over. This, some argue, limits the attacking potential of the West Indies, who have dominated world cricket since the 1980s. After the success of Australia's pace pair, Dennis Lillee and Jeff Thompson, in the 1970s, the West Indies learnt that by bowling four pace bowlers in rotation they could blast most teams into submission. The cricket purists and, more importantly, the other often-beaten cricket nations, did not like this one-dimensional approach, and forced the change through the International Cricket Council, the ruling body of world cricket.

England versus
Australia for the
Ashes.

with the legendary W.G. Grace playing. After the match the *Sporting Times* told its readers of the 'death of English cricket', adding that 'the body will be cremated and the ashes taken to Australia'. The Ashes (from a stump burnt during the England tour of Australia in 1883) are now kept in an urn at the museum at Lord's.

The first women's cricket club was formed in England in 1887, and women in Australia and New Zealand took up the game soon after. Test matches are now played between England, Australia, New Zealand and the West Indies, and there is a World Cup competition for women. The current holders are England.

Since the 1970s the game has been modernized and brought into the 'television age'. This is due in no small part to the efforts of Kerry

Pakistan captain Imran Khan after the teams brilliant victory over England in the 1992 World Cup final.

Packer, an Australian press and TV magnate. He shook the cricket establishment by attracting top players to his 'World Series Cricket'. This offered big money to the players and a world-wide television deal. The international boards finally got their players back, but the game, and the players' expectations and rewards, had now joined other sports in the big-money league.

During this time the stars of world

cricket became household names, and nowadays even people who are not sport fans have heard of Ian Botham and Viv Richards.

Cricket now has an official World Cup, which is played every four years. There are night matches, white balls and coloured clothing – all once part of the 'Kerry Packer Circus' – as part of its spectacle. Cricket traditionalists despair of these changes to their great game, but there is little doubt that the cricketing public prefer to watch this type of fast, all-action cricket.

As the money at stake grows through sponsorship deals and advertising, and as personal satellite dishes link the world, there is little doubt that more changes are to come. Even now, when international matches are played, cricket fans all around the world can sit down at different times of their days and nights to watch live coverage of their favourite sport.

Major Competitions

International

- ○ World Cup (Men's)   Held every four years. From 1996, twelve teams will compete.
- ○ World Cup (Women's)   Held every four years. Eight teams compete.

Domestic

- ○ Australia – Sheffield Shield, with six states competing in a league system.
- ○ England – County Championship, with eighteen major counties competing in the men's league championship and eleven in the women's.
- ○ India – Ranji Trophy, with twenty-seven teams competing in zonal groups and the winners playing off for a place in the final.
- ○ New Zealand – Shell Trophy, with six districts competing in a league system.
- ○ Pakistan – Quaid-e-Azam Trophy, with eight regional sides competing for a place in the final.
- ○ South Africa – Currie Cup, with six states competing in a league system.
- ○ Sri Lanka – P. Saravanamuttu Trophy, with eleven teams competing for a place in the final.
- ○ West Indies – Red Stripe Cup, with six teams competing in a league system.

ABOUT THE GAME

Apart from winning or losing, a team can tie or draw a cricket match. A tie happens when the team batting second scores the same number of runs as the team batting first. A draw happens when the team batting second has scored fewer runs than the team batting first but still has some of its eleven batsmen in hand at the end of the game.

There are a number of ways for a batting team to score runs: hitting the ball over the boundary for four or six runs; hitting the ball and taking one, two, three or more runs; byes (when the wicketkeeper misses the ball and the batsmen take one or more runs); leg byes (when the ball comes off a part of the batsman other than the hand holding the bat); wides; and no-balls. A wide is called when the bowler bowls a ball that, in the

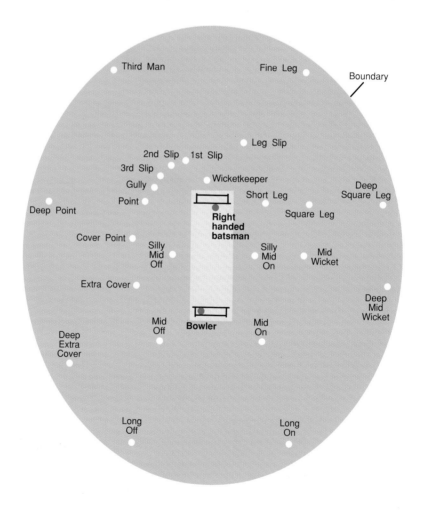

Fielding positions to a right-handed batsman.

Boundary – Six

Bye

Short run

No ball

Boundary – Four

Dead ball

Out

Wide

Leg-bye

umpire's opinion, the batsman couldn't hit from his or her normal stance. A no-ball can be called for a number of reasons – the main ones are explained in the Basic Rules section on page 45 of this book. The batting side are awarded one run for a wide and – in most forms of cricket – a no-ball. In some matches, two runs are given for a no-ball.

Most cricket matches are played outdoors on grass, but a lot of youth cricket is played on artificial wickets. These are pitches made of plastic or rubber matting, which is very hard-wearing. Many cricketers also play indoor cricket during the winter. These games are often six-a-side.

There are two main types of cricket match – 'limited overs' and 'declaration' games. Limited overs matches are often league or cup games, while declaration games are usually friendlies. In a declaration game, the team batting first stop their innings either when they have been bowled out or when they think they have set a large enough target to win the match. The team batting second then have the remaining time to either beat this target and win, or draw by not losing all of their wickets. If they are bowled out for a lower score than the team batting first, they lose.

Matches in which teams have two innings each and take three, four or five days to complete usually take place only in professional cricket. Test matches between countries, which last for five days, are the longest games.

Umpiring signals

BATTING SKILLS

Most players can be taught the correct way to play the various batting shots, or strokes. Batsmen of most standards will, at some time or another, play a stroke just like Ian Botham, Viv Richards or Mohammed Azharuddin. The problem is that most batsmen either can't play each shot correctly every time, or choose the wrong ball to play a shot to.

Shot selection and timing are the two most important factors in batting. Although these are often natural gifts, they can both be improved through net and match practice. Watching top players will also help. Notice how they quickly decide what stroke they intend to play to a certain ball so that they can get into position to execute the shot.

Pride of India, Sachin Tendulkar, plays another glorious drive.

Grip, stance and backlift

T hese are the fundamentals of batting. The top players concentrate on these three things more than any others. They know that if these aren't right, their batting will suffer.

○ **Grip:** Hold the bat with your hands close together near the top of the handle, and the top hand gripping tighter than the bottom. The V-shapes made by your thumbs and first fingers should be in line with each other and pointing somewhere between the splice and the outside edge.

○ **Stance:** Stand with your feet about a bat's width apart, and your weight evenly balanced on both feet. Put one foot each side of the batting crease, and bend your knees slightly to keep tension out of the body. Rest your hands comfortably against the front thigh, with the back of the top hand facing extra cover.

Your front shoulder should be pointing at the bowler, and your eyes should be level, over middle stump and both looking at the bowler's hand. If a right-handed bowler is bowling round the wicket or a left-arm bowler

A perfect stance. Graham Gooch has his feet comfortably apart, his weight evenly balanced and his head still. His high and straight backlift allows him the time and power to play any shot.

Finally, if you want to be a consistent batsman you must develop the ability to concentrate. Many players lose their wicket to a bad ball by lifting their head and taking their eye off the ball. Another common fault among players is moving their feet before they have picked up the line and length of the ball. If there is one piece of advice that could improve most batsmen's play, it is: stand still and commit yourself to the stroke as late as possible.

is bowling over the wicket, open up your stance slightly. This is so you can see his or her approach and delivery with both eyes.

○ **Backlift:** A high, straight backlift is essential to get over the ball and keep it down, and also to generate power. The wrists should move back and up, and there should be no movement of the head or feet. More and more top players lift their bat early and hold it there. However, most batsmen get a better rhythm by lifting it just as the bowler starts his or her delivery stride.

Front-foot shots

○ **Forward defence:** This is one shot that every batsman should be able to play. It is played to a good-length ball in line with the stumps or just outside off stump. The aim of the shot is to stop the ball dead.

Your front shoulder and head, not your foot, should lead into the stroke. Your foot should then follow naturally, and should be placed just inside the line of the ball. Control the bat with your top hand, and keep your front elbow high. Grip the bat lightly with

Get past that! Allan Border's forward defence shows the bat and pad together, weight over bent front leg, eyes still and level, and top hand in control.

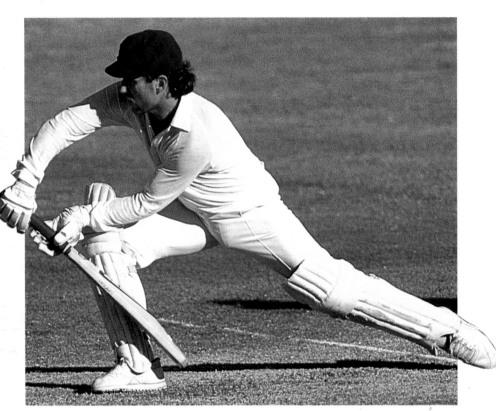

the thumb and forefinger of the bottom hand. Ease up on to the inside big toe of the back foot to really get over the ball.

○ **The drive:** There is no more satisfying shot in cricket – for batsman and spectator alike – than the perfectly executed drive. This attacking shot is played to a half volley, and can be played with a full or a checked swing. When using a checked swing, the batsman allows the bat to follow through only until it is horizontal, giving more control but less power.

 Four runs! David Boon drives with a checked swing for greater control. The high front elbow will make sure that the ball has gone along the ground.

 Jan Brittin of England has a perfect follow-through after a great off drive. Her eyes are level and her weight is on the front foot.

Imran Khan
sweeps during the
1992 World Cup
final. His back
knee has dropped
to play the shot,
his pad is in line
with the ball and
his head is still.
Perfect.

The three main drives are the off drive, the on drive and the cover drive. The drive starts like the forward defensive shot, with the head and front shoulder leading the front foot alongside the line of the ball. Then the full face of the bat comes down the line of the stroke, hitting the ball on the half volley. Your head and weight should be over your front leg, and the top hand should be in control. For the on drive, dip your front shoulder into the shot and open up your front foot to point toward mid-on. The top hand should be in control of the shot. Don't try to hit the ball too hard.

○ **The sweep:** This attacking shot

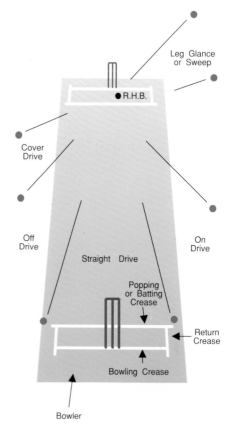

Range of Front Foot Strokes

is played to a good-length ball that is going down leg side or a ball that has pitched outside leg stump and is turning in. In both cases you shouldn't be in danger of being given out lbw. Don't attempt to play this shot to a spinner if the wicket is too bouncy.

Start the stroke as though playing the forward defensive. Make contact with the ball just after it pitches, and aim to hit the ball between square leg and fine leg. Bend the front leg so that the back knee touches or nearly touches the ground. If you miss the ball with the bat, your front pad should stop it. The reverse sweep is a dangerous shot that should be left to a batsman such as Mike Gatting.

Back-foot shots

○ **The pull:** This is a very aggressive attacking shot, and is played to a short ball or 'long hop' that is missing the stumps on the leg side. If the ball bounces above chest height, don't try to play this or any other shot, as it's very difficult to control the ball. Nor should you attempt this shot against a fast bowler.

Take your back foot outside the off stump, with the toes pointing toward

mid-off. Move the front foot back to the leg side, so that the weight ends up on this leg. Try to play the ball at arm's length for maximum power and control. Don't let your head rock back toward the stumps, and make sure you watch the ball right on to your bat. You should be aiming to hit the ball between square leg and mid-wicket.

○ **Back defence:** This is played to a ball that is just short of a length on the stumps or in the 'channel of uncertainty' just outside off stump. You should try to stop the ball dead by having a firm yet relaxed grip. If played well, this is infuriating for quick bowlers, as all their effort seems wasted.

Take your back foot back parallel

Beautifully controlled back defence against a quick bowler. Mohammed Azharuddin gets right back, stays perfectly sideways-on, has a very high front elbow and therefore controls the ball down.

Pure grace and power. Richie Richardson's square cut shows the importance of weight transfer to the back foot and a full follow-through.

to the crease so that your head moves in line with the ball. Bring the front foot back alongside it so that the body remains side-on. If you get chest-on and the ball rises sharply, you won't be able to duck or sway out of the way, and you could get hit. Keep your head well forward, with your weight over your body.

Control the bat with your top hand, and keep the bat very straight with a high front elbow. A light thumb and forefinger grip helps to keep the face of the bat slanted downward. Keep the bat close to your body, and don't follow through.

○ **Square cut:** This is an exhilarating shot, especially against quick bowlers, and is played to a short ball wide of off stump.

Martin Crowe makes the forcing shot off the back foot look so easy. His head remains forward, the bottom hand punches through the line of the ball and the bat finishes in a horizontal position.

To play this shot well, turn your front shoulder to get really sideways-on, and take the back foot back and well across to the leg side. You also need to play the ball at arm's length, with the weight ending up on the back leg.

○ **Forcing shot**: This is played to a ball that is short of a length and missing the wicket. It is a good scoring shot on a wicket with regular bounce, and is relatively safe if played with a checked swing. The ball can be hit to anywhere from cover to wide mid-on.

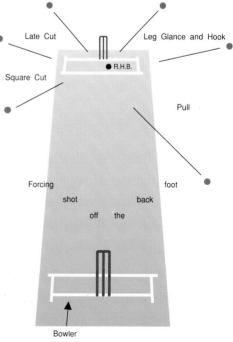

Late Cut

Leg Glance and Hook

R.H.B.

Square Cut

Pull

Forcing shot off the back foot

Bowler

Range of Back Foot Strokes

19

Move into position in the same way as you do for the back defence but, instead of stopping the ball, 'punch' it by pushing your bottom hand through just before impact. Your weight is mainly on your back foot, but keep your balance by leaving the head forward.

Running between the wickets

T he most annoying way to be dismissed is by being run out, as it's nearly always the batsmen's fault. If you follow these basic rules you should avoid it happening to you or your partner.

○　Call before you set off: 'Yes' if you want to run, 'No' if you don't. It is up to the striker to call if the ball goes anywhere in front of him or her. The non-striker should call if the ball goes behind, that is between square point and square leg.

○　If you are the non-striker, 'back up' by starting to move down the pitch as the bowler delivers the ball.

○　Always slide the bat over the crease as you complete a run.

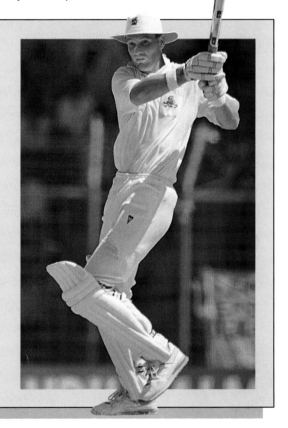

Key points for successful batting

○　*Don't attempt to play shots that you have not got right in practice.*

○　*Play yourself in. Give your reflexes time to adjust to the conditions.*

○　*At the start of an innings, shorten your backlift to give you more time.*

○　*Leave balls that won't hit your stumps and you don't want to score from.*

○　*Try to keep the ball on the ground. More people are out caught than any other way.*

○　*When playing different types of bowling, bear in mind the following guidelines. For fast bowling, move back; for swing bowling, play late; for spin bowling, move forward.*

○　*Remember, the successful batsman is not the one who plays the most good shots but the one who plays the fewest bad shots.*

BOWLING SKILLS

Would you like to face Curtley Ambrose of the West Indies?

Coaches and commentators often say that bowlers should bowl a good line and length. Bowling a good line means aiming the ball so that it pitches either on line with the stumps or just outside off stump. A good-length ball is a ball that makes the batsman unsure whether to play forward or back. If you bowl a good line and length, batsmen will find it difficult to score without playing risky shots. If they miss the ball, you have a good chance of bowling them out.

C ricket is a battle of wits between batsman and bowler, and if you are the bowler, you start with the upper hand, because you can decide on the line, length and type of ball bowled. You can only keep on top, however, if you have enough control to bowl the ball where you want it. This control can come only from lots of practice.

Whatever type of bowler you are, you should try to develop a variety of deliveries. You can try bowling slower and quicker balls, and also use the width of the crease to alter your angle of attack. All of these things can make a batsman misjudge a ball and, along with well-thought-out field placings, can help you think out as well as bowl out the opposing batsmen. The basis for successful bowling is a good grip, run-up, delivery and follow-through.

England's Jo Chamberlain gets great height in her delivery stride. This, along with her very good sideways position, makes her a top international pace bowler.

○ **Grip:** How you hold the ball varies for different types of bowling, and each individual bowler can adjust the basic grip to suit him or her. The basic grip is to have the first and second fingers each side of the seam on top of the ball, with your thumb on the seam under the ball. Hold the ball firmly but gently in the fingers – not the palm.

○ **Run-up:** This should be smooth and not too long. Fix your eyes on the stumps and watch this point right through to your follow-through. Try varying the length, speed and angle of run-up until you find the style that suits you.

○ **Delivery:** As you reach the wicket, get sideways-on by swinging your front arm high across your body while jumping slightly in the air. While looking behind this arm at the stumps, lean back to give yourself extra power. Your weight is on the back foot, and your front arm is thrown out in front of you toward the batsman.

As your front leg lands, your bowling arm should be high and straight. Keep your eyes as level as possible as you release the ball. Your bowling arm follows through, swinging across your body so that the shoulder of your bowling arm points down the wicket.

○ **Follow-through:** After releasing the ball, continue down the pitch for a few paces to keep your rhythm and momentum. A good follow-through also helps to prevent injury by absorbing the impact of your bowling action.

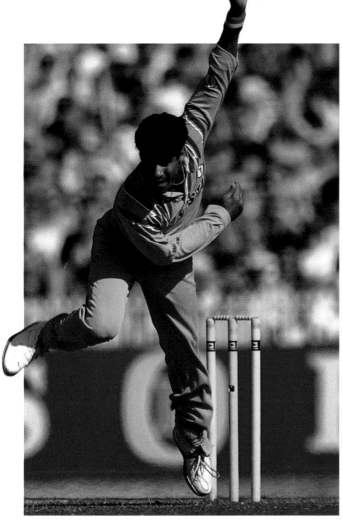

○ **Swing bowling:** You can make a ball swing in the air using three methods: shining the side of the ball you don't want the ball to swing toward; holding the seam of the ball upright and pointing it slightly toward the side where you want the ball to swing; or changing your bowling action.

All of these will help the ball to swing, as long as you keep your wrist firm behind the ball as you deliver it and don't let the wrist twist to either side. Pitch the ball well up to give it time to swing.

○ **Outswing:** The outswinger swings in the air toward the slips when bowled to a right-handed batsman. The seam should be pointing toward the slips, with the shiny side toward leg side. Try to

What an action! Waqar Younis shows what has made him one of the most feared bowlers in the world. His front arm and bowling arm follow through powerfully but his eyes stay level for maximum control.

Types of delivery

○ **Fast:** The genuine fast bowler is rare, for the ability to bowl quickly can't be learnt. If you have the ability but not much control, following the guidelines above should make you a very effective wicket-taking and match-winning bowler. Be careful not to over-bowl, as you risk stress injuries and a loss of pace.

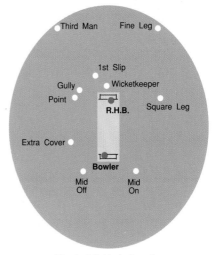

Standard field placings for a right-handed outswing bowler

make your bowling action as side-on as possible, and follow through fully with the bowling arm to the off side of your front leg.

○ **Inswing:** The inswinger swings in the air from off to leg, when bowled to a right-handed batsman. The seam should point toward fine leg, with the shiny side toward the off side. To bowl an effective inswinger you need to be more chest-on than normal, looking inside your front arm rather than behind it. Follow through with your bowling arm to the leg side of your front leg.

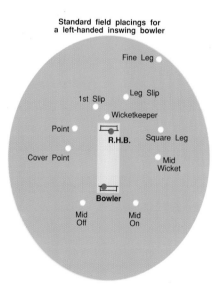

Standard field placings for a left-handed inswing bowler

○ **Seam bowling:** A seam bowler attempts to make the ball pitch on a vertical seam and thus deviate off the ground. The grip is the same as the basic grip and, as with swing bowling, needs a firm wrist behind the ball.

○ **Spin bowling:** A cunning, patient and accurate bowler who can spin the ball is as much of a match winner as the pace bowler. You'll probably be hit for more boundaries than other bowlers, but you'll also get more wickets. Remember to toss the ball up when you bowl spin. Without this 'flight' the ball won't spin.

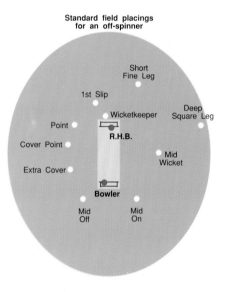

Standard field placings for an off-spinner

○ **Off-spin:** This is a delivery that turns from the off to the leg. The top joint of your first finger grips across the seam of the ball, and this becomes the main spinning finger. The second finger, which should be well spaced away from the first, also grips across the seam with the thumb lying along

the seam.

The spin is given by the wrist being cocked back and then snapped forward, with the first finger dragging down on the seam in a clockwise direction. Pivot on a braced front leg to impart more spin, then throw your bowling arm out toward the batsman, following through outside the front leg.

○ **Leg-spin:** This delivery turns from the leg to the off, and is the type of bowling that many batsmen can't play very well. Leg-spin is more difficult to control than off-spin, and is used most often as attacking bowling, aiming to take wickets rather than save runs. It's great fun to bowl and great fun to watch.

For the leg break, the first two fingers cradle the ball, with the third finger bent along the seam. This is the main spinning finger. The spin is given by the wrist being cocked back and the third finger dragging the seam in an anticlockwise direction. A good sideways action is still needed, but the delivery stride should be longer than the off-spinner's. You'll get more bounce and accuracy with a high bowling arm, but you'll get more spin with a slightly lower one.

Shane Warne bowling during Australia's tour of England in 1993. Warne was Australia's leading wicket-taker in the Ashes series and showed how leg-spin bowling can mesmerize even top-class batsmen.

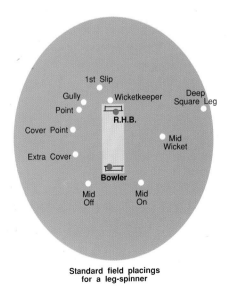

Standard field placings
for a leg-spinner

25

WICKETKEEPING

A s wicketkeeper, you are involved in the action more than any other fielder. You must be ready for every ball bowled in case the batsman misses it, and you have to collect every throw from the fielders. Most importantly, you take more wickets than any other player, with catches, run-outs and stumpings.

Stance

T he most common position is the squatting position, with the weight on the balls of the feet. Keep your feet comfortably apart, with the knees bent and the seat well down. The hands should be together between the knees, fingers pointing down with the palms facing the bowler. Most importantly, keep your head still and your eyes level.

Position

W hen standing up to the wicket, keep your inside foot in line with the off stump and move close

 Javed Miandad plays a risky reverse sweep, but Alec Stewart takes no chances. He stays down until the ball bounces and keeps his eyes on the ball.

Equipment

○ **Gloves:** *These should be large enough to fit comfortably on a hand wearing an inner glove, and loose enough to be removed quickly for a throw. They should also be small enough for the fingers to move all of the glove. 'Break in' new gloves before wearing them in a match. Lay the glove face up and hammer the toe of an old bat into the palm. This takes the stiffness out of gloves and makes catching easier.*

All wicketkeepers should wear 'inners' as well. These thin leather or cotton inner gloves are worn as extra protection for the hands. Most keepers wet their inners before putting them on. This is to make them flexible and give the glove a better 'feel'. This is particularly important for slow bowlers.

○ **Pads:** *Many keepers use short pads with no protection above the knee. These make moving about easier and remove the risk of your gloves getting caught in your pads. Make sure they are light and not too bulky.*

○ **Other equipment:** *Like every male cricketer, keepers should wear an athletic support with a pocket that contains a protector or 'box'. Other things to remember are always to have available a cap or hat to keep the sun out of your eyes, and not to wear boots with studs that are too long. These can restrict your foot movement by getting stuck in the turf when turning or pivoting.*

enough so that your gloves are resting no more than 15 cm behind the line of the stumps. This should give you a clear view of the delivery of the ball and also make sure that you're close enough to attempt a stumping.

When standing up, don't move too early. Give yourself time to pick up the line and length of the ball. Come up as the ball bounces. If the ball stays low, your hands remain low rather than coming up and then having to move down again. Don't move back; this will take you out of range for a stumping.

Move your hands together as much as possible, and go for a one-handed catch only when you can't reach with two. Try to take the ball with your arms straight and relaxed. Then you can 'give' as you take the ball by bending the elbows. This stops the ball bouncing out and reduces the risk of injuring your hands.

When standing back to faster bowlers, don't stand directly behind the stumps, but keep your inside foot aligned with off stump in the same way as you would when standing up. For left-handed bowlers you might need to stand a little wider so that you get a clear view of the delivery.

When standing back, don't stand too close to the stumps. You should look to take the ball between your knees and your waist just as the ball begins to drop in its trajectory. Don't move until the ball has left the bowler's

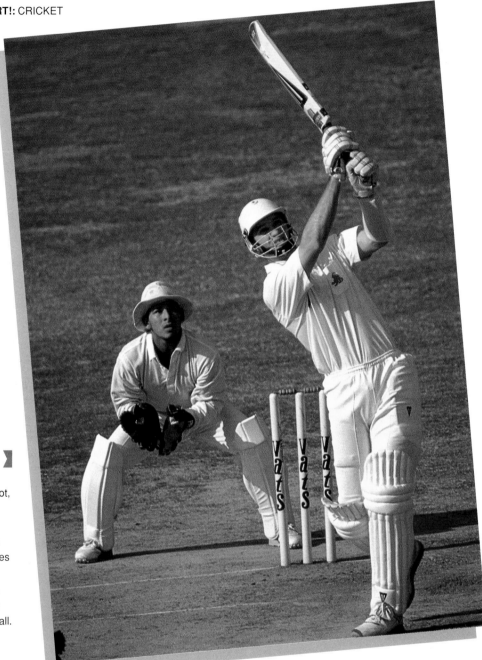

An excellent shot, but look at the keeper's great position. India's Keiran More rises with the ball, hands together, should Graham Hick miss the ball. I don't think he did!

hand – you don't want to be wrong-footed by moving too early. Keep your knees bent so that you can move quickly one way or the other.

Don't use your pads to stop awkward balls; always try to get your gloves to the ball. Once the batsman has hit the ball, immediately get in behind the stumps ready for the fielder's throw and possible run-out.

FIELDING SKILLS

All players should give as much thought to fielding as they do to their batting and bowling. Practise your fielding skills and learn to concentrate and be aggressive. A captain can then set a defensive or attacking field and know that the bowlers will get the back-up they need.

Good fielding can put pressure on even the best batsmen and force them to do something that they didn't want to do and give away their wicket. It is a good idea to become a specialist in one or two positions. You might then find that you become as invaluable to your team for your fielding as others are for their batting and bowling.

Attacking interception

When fielding in the infield or close to the bat, the one-handed interception is the quickest way to pick up the ball and attempt to run someone out.

Run toward the ball, getting low before you reach it. Pick it up outside the right foot (left foot for left-handers)

This will be close. Craig McDermott shows the importance of staying low when picking up one-handed. Gordon Greenidge is ready to run his bat along the ground to avoid being run out.

Great throwing technique from Philip Defreitas. Weight on the back foot ready to transfer over the front foot and front arm pointing at the target. His head is still and his throwing arm is bent, ready to power the ball in.

and, in one movement and still on the run, throw the ball underarm at the stumps or wicketkeeper.

From further out, the fielder should look to take the ball two-handed in front of the right foot (the left foot for a left-hander), which is at right angles to the line of the ball. This gets the body side-on ready for a fast, flat throw. Throws from the outfield should be aimed at the top of the stumps.

Defensive interception

This is often called the long barrier, and the first priority with this technique is to stop the ball. Once you have run toward the ball and are in line with it, bend your left knee to the ground at right angles to the line of the ball. The right foot should then go alongside the knee to make a 'long barrier'. The hands are together, with the palms facing the ball and the eyes watching the ball right into the hands. As you stand up from this position you are naturally sideways-on and ready to throw.

Retrieving

If the ball is hit past you when you are fielding, there are two ways to retrieve it. Both types of retrieval aim to pick up the ball on the run and return it quickly to the wicketkeeper. The first is the pick-up and throw on the turn, and is used when the ball is hit just past the close fielders or infield. The key to doing this successfully is to pick up the ball outside the right foot (left foot for left-handers) and to throw the ball as you

Throwing

Fast, accurate throwing is one of the most important skills in cricket. Every fielder should be able to throw accurately to save runs, to put pressure on the batsmen and, if this is done really well, to get run-outs. In good teams every throw is also 'backed up' by a fielder at both the wicketkeeper's and the bowler's end, to prevent overthrows.

Catching

A good catch inspires a team, but a dropped catch inspires the batsman. To maintain a high success rate in catching you need to practise as much as you do for your batting and bowling. Before practising, you must master the correct techniques, otherwise you risk injury. There are three main types of catch – high, close and skim.

When making a high catch, move into position as soon as you sight the ball. Try to be stationary as you catch the ball, with your head still. Catch the ball above eye level, and 'give' with the ball to absorb the impact.

He won't drop this – eyes on the ball, hands together and away from the body. David Gower makes catching look easy.

jump and turn.

If the ball is hit further past the fielders, the pick-up is still outside the right foot but, instead of throwing as you jump and turn, you use your right foot to push off. This gives you more power for the long throw.

CAPTAINCY

I n no other sport is the captain so important as in cricket. You can make the game rewarding and fun for everyone, or you can make it boring and even put people off the game. You may not necessarily be the best player. Mike Brearley captained a successful England team without really being good enough as a player to merit regular inclusion. What he did have was natural leadership skills, a great tactical awareness and, perhaps most importantly of all, the ability to get the most from his players.

The key things to remember as a captain are that most people play better after encouragement, not criticism, and that a bad sporting attitude spoils everyone's enjoyment.

The toss

I f you win the toss, it is your decision whether to bat first or second. This decision can often depend on your team's ability to chase a set target. If they perform better when setting a target and then defending it, this might influence a captain to try to bat first as often as possible.

As a general rule, a pitch tends to help spinners as the game progresses, due to the surface being roughed up and therefore helping the ball grip and turn. A lot of grass on the pitch tends to help pace bowlers to move the ball off the wicket, and an overcast sky is said to aid swing bowling. A wet pitch can help all the bowlers to get movement, but can make fielding and bowling treacherous.

Fielding

A short team talk before going out to field is often a good idea, as you can focus your players' minds and talk through any tactical plans you may have.

Early on you will be making adjustments for the pace of the wicket and outfield and the form of the bowlers and batsmen. You don't want a field that is too attacking and lets the opposition get off to a flying start, but you do want their early batsmen to feel under pressure from your field placings. Don't set over-attacking fields to spinners; it's demoralizing for any bowler to be hit all around the ground.

Remember not to over-bowl your opening bowlers; batsmen get used to a bowler if he or she bowls for long enough. Also, don't use your spinners as a last resort – you'd be surprised how many top-order batsmen struggle against spin bowling.

Know how long your bowlers like to bowl for – some like several short spells and some like one long spell. And remember that you can't set a field for bad bowling, but you can always try another bowler. But let your bowlers know what tactics you're following so they can bowl accordingly.

Although you shouldn't waste time, always be ready to change the field for different batsmen. This is why fielders should always keep an eye on their captain when the ball is dead. Remember, always be prepared to try something different if the game is stagnating or not going the way you planned.

Batting

Y ou obviously have less influence on your team when they're batting, but there are things that you as captain can do.

The pressure is on Keppler Wessells, but not just to win the toss. This is South Africa's historic first test in the West Indies after their re-admittance to international cricket.

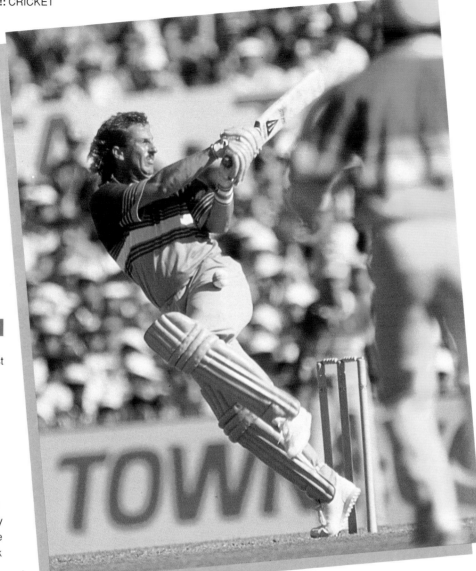

▶ ▶ ▶ ▶

England's greatest ever player? Ian Botham was the player that opposition teams feared more than any other. A middle-order batsman in test matches, he often opened in one-day matches to get the team off to a quick start.

Firstly, set a batting order. This might mean moving a player up the order if you need quick runs. You can also change the order once the innings is under way. If you do this, tell the batsmen concerned why you are doing it.

Try to have a word with each batsman as he or she goes out to bat, for encouragement and to let him or her know what is expected. Try as much as possible to let each player bat in his or her own style.

Finally, never declare so late that the opposition don't have at least a sporting chance of achieving their target.

FITNESS TRAINING

You should be fit before playing cricket. This is not only to avoid injury, but also so that you perform to the best of your ability.

The elements of fitness

Fitness has six elements: stamina, muscular endurance, flexibility, speed, power and strength. You should concentrate on improving all of these if you want to make the most of your natural ability. Below are the types of exercises that you can do to improve each of these elements. Many professional players are now using a combination of all these types of training to keep at the top of their game.

○ **Stamina:** All-over body exercises such as swimming, cycling

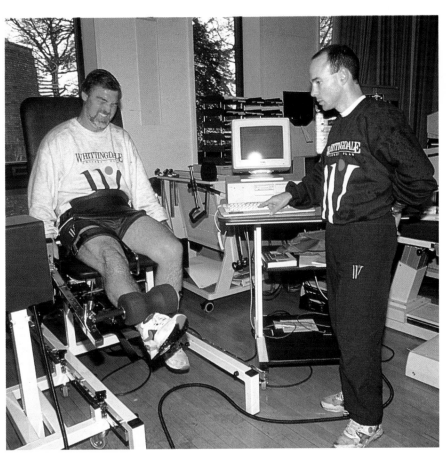

Top players nowadays work on their fitness almost as much as their cricket. Here, Mike Gatting tests his leg strength before England's 1993 tour to India.

35

and particularly running, as it's the most relevant to cricket, are all good for improving your stamina. Do these for twenty minutes or more at least three times a week.

○ **Muscular endurance:** This is the ability of a muscle or muscle group to repeat exercises such as sit-ups, press-ups or pull-ups. Start by doing ten of each of these, and increase the number as your muscular endurance improves. Muscular endurance can also be improved by training with light weights.

○ **Flexibility:** Many cricketers are inflexible, as they neglect this part of fitness training. This means that they are more likely to pick up injuries, the effectiveness of other areas of fitness training is reduced, and the development of cricket skills can be reduced. Get into the habit of going through the stretching exercises shown here for at least

Stretching exercises that will reduce the risk of injury. From top to bottom: side stretch; shoulder stretch; wrist stretch; lying stretch.

five minutes before and after any exercise. This will stop you from getting stiff.

○ **Speed:** Speed is important, not only for bowlers who want to bowl fast or fielders who want to run people out, but also for batsmen. This is particularly true against fast bowling, when you not only want to react quickly to see where the ball is, but also to respond quickly to hit it. Batsmen such as David Gower, who think and move quickly, seem to have a lot of time to play their shot, and often look very stylish because of this.

Speed of reaction and response can be improved by a combination of power, strength and flexibility exercises and by practice against quick bowlers. Sprinting is also a good general speed exercise.

○ **Strength and power:** The most common way to improve strength and power is weight training. This

From top to bottom: calf stretch; hamstring and lower back stretch; hip stretch; groin stretch. Ease into each stretch and don't over-stretch.

Good running between the wickets by Graham Gooch and Hugh Morris comes from fitness and practice.

stimulates the growth and development of muscles by increasing the resistance placed on them. If you do this sort of training you should find that you can bowl faster, hit the ball further and generally move more quickly.

The exercises you need to do are specific to different parts of your body, and you can concentrate on, for instance, arm and shoulder weight training if you want to improve the speed and distance of your throwing.

Before starting this potentially dangerous training, get advice from your coach. This will make sure that you are doing the correct exercises for cricket in a safe way. Make sure that you warm up before and after training, to prevent injury. This should involve a gentle jog and then a range of stretches. Don't over-train; if you feel any pain or start to feel dizzy, stop.

SKILL TRAINING

Batting

If you're trying to learn a new batting shot or improve on one that you don't play very well, follow the sequence below. It is best to watch your coach or a video of a top player performing the skill you are trying to improve. You can then copy what you have seen.

In front of a mirror, try to improve one point at a time, starting with the backlift and then watching the feet, legs, shoulders, arms and, most importantly, the head. Keep repeating the shot until you have got the 'shape' and rhythm right.

Then get a friend to throw a ball, gently at first, in a way that you can practise the shot. Keep repeating this until you are happy that you have mastered the stroke. This type of practice is called 'grooving'.

Now is the time for net practice, which is a realistic way of practising batting shots, as you have to select

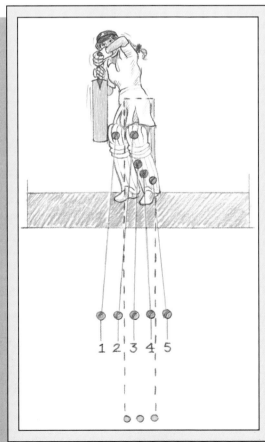

The LBW Law

1 NOT OUT The ball pitches outside the dotted area between wicket and wicket and hits the striker outside the off-stump. If the striker plays no shot and the ball would have hit the wicket, the striker would be out.
2 OUT The ball pitches outside the dotted area, but would have hit the wicket – it must not be passing over the top of the stumps.
3 OUT The ball pitches inside the dotted area and would have hit the wicket.
4 OUT The ball pitches inside the dotted area and would not have passed outside the off stump.
5 NOT OUT A ball pitching outside the leg stump is not out.

39

Chris Lewis forgets the first rule of net safety – never practice on an airport runway!

when to play a particular shot. If you are lucky enough to have access to a bowling machine, this is a good time to use it. Don't be tempted to have it bowling too fast, as this is poor practice and can be dangerous.

Net practice can be dangerous. Always remember the following safety points:

❍ When bowling, always face the batsman; the ball could be hit out at any time.

❍ Recover the ball from the side netting with the end of your bat. You can easily be hit by the batsman next door if you get too close to the netting.

❍ Don't mess about; bat and bowl as you would in a match.

Bowling

Practise your bowling by starting with the run-up and then moving on to the turn or 'bound' as you approach the wicket. You should then concentrate on each element of the delivery and the follow-through until you've got them right.

You can start by bowling at three stumps and then, to really test your accuracy, try bowling at just one. You can also see if you are bowling a good length by putting a handkerchief on the ground on a good length and line and seeing if you can hit it.

In net practice, always try and bowl a good line and length.

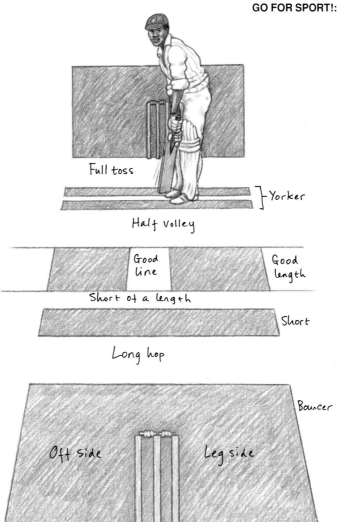

Full toss

Yorker

Half volley

Good line

Good length

Short of a length

Short

Long hop

Bouncer

Off side

Leg side

Wicketkeeping

T he first type of practice you want to try is without a batsman in position. This gives you the chance to try to improve elements of your technique without distraction.

To start with, work on off side takes, then leg side, then a random selection. Ask the person who is feeding the ball to vary the length. Once you are happy with your feet, body, hands and head positions, get a batsman to join your practice. He or she should bat with a stump, deliberately playing and missing the ball to make the practice more realistic. You can then continue this practice in a net with the batsman batting properly.

Robin Smith takes a brilliant reflex catch to dismiss Moin Khan. To move this quickly you must have your knees bent, weight forward and hands ready. Try and do these things when you practise close catching.

Fielding

Fielding practice is often neglected, but should include close catching, high catching, stopping and retrieving the ball, and throwing.

Start your catching practice with someone throwing the ball to you, or by throwing a ball against a wall. Then make it more realistic by having someone hit the ball to you with a bat so that it comes to you at different speeds and heights. Finally, practise on the pitch with the ball coming to you as it would in a match.

When practising any cricket skills, it is worth remembering the following points:

- Warm up before you start.
- Start by using a soft ball to get the technique right, then move on to a hard ball.
- Don't over-practise, as skills start to break down.
- None of these skills will come straight away. You need to work at them regularly until you do them automatically without thinking about them.
- Try to watch your local county team warm up before a county match. You'll see that they never stop practising these skills, and you might pick up a few new ideas that you can try.

EQUIPMENT

Bats

Most people use a bat that is too heavy. This means that they don't have full control, and their batting suffers. Select a bat that you can pick up in a backlift and use to play any shot with just your top hand. If you can't do this you will have trouble adjusting the bat at the last moment, should the ball deviate.

If you are buying a bat, don't buy one that is too expensive. Some of the mid-price and lower-price bats will serve you just as well as plastic-coated bats. However, these need less attention than a natural wood bat, which needs regular light oiling with raw linseed oil. Cracks also need sanding with a fine sandpaper and sometimes gluing with wood glue.

All bats should be 'broken in' with an old ball before being used. This is to harden the bat up and reduce the chance of it cracking.

Protection

○ **Pads:** These should be light, with straps that don't flap about. They

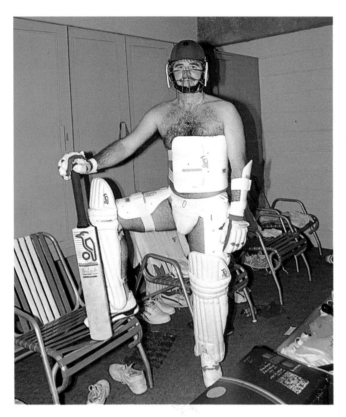

Has Allan Lamb forgotten anything? Pads, gloves, thigh pads, chest protector, box and helmet – it all seems to be there.

More and more players are wearing zinc cream or sun-block to protect themselves against harmful rays from the sun.

must also be easy to run in. A light, non-bulky thigh pad can offer good extra protection and added confidence on a bouncy pitch or against quick bowling. Chest guards, arm guards and second thigh pads are all worn by many top players, but they're not necessary for young players.

○ **Batting gloves:** These should fit snugly but not tightly. They should not be over-padded, as this will restrict movement.

○ **Box:** A box should always be worn by male players who are using a hard ball. It is best held in place by an athletic support with a pocket.

○ **Helmet:** County and international players would be foolish not to wear a helmet against the quickest bowlers in the world. More and more club players wear them for confidence as much as anything. They are not needed in schools, or colts' cricket.

Clothing

All clothing should be loose-fitting to allow a full range of movement, but shouldn't be baggy as it could get caught up when batting. A short- and a long-sleeved sweater are advisable, as is a cap or hat to protect the eyes from the glare of the sun.

○ **Footwear:** Spiked boots are a must for most grounds. Shock-absorbing insoles can help to prevent stiff or sore legs, especially for fast bowlers.

BASIC RULES

You are out lbw:

❍ If any part of you (except the hands holding the bat) is hit by a ball that pitches wicket to wicket.

❍ If the ball pitches on the off side but hits part of you in the area from wicket to wicket.

❍ If the ball was a full toss and the point of impact was in a straight line between wicket and wicket.

❍ If the ball pitched outside off stump and the point of impact was outside off stump but you weren't attempting a shot.

However, you are out only if the following three criteria are met as well:

❍ It was a fair delivery.

❍ In the opinion of the umpire, the ball would have hit the stumps.

❍ The ball didn't hit the bat or hands holding the bat first.

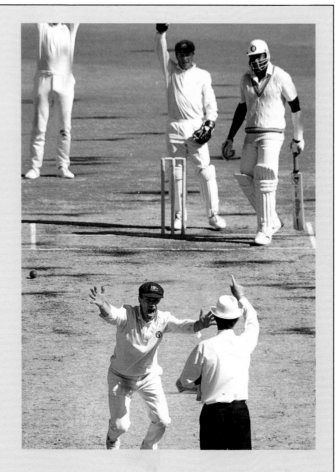

 Devon Malcolm out lbw. Greg Matthews is perhaps a little too excitable in claiming the wicket of this top batsman.

These are the main reasons for the umpire calling a no-ball:

❍ The bowler has no part of his or her front foot behind the batting crease.

❍ The bowler's back foot is touching or outside the return crease.

❍ The fielding team have more than two fielders behind square on the leg side.

❍ The bowler did not tell the umpire whether he or she would bowl over or around the wicket.

❍ The bowler straightened his or her arm during the part of the delivery swing that directly preceded the ball leaving the hand.

A wide is a delivery that the umpire thinks the batsman can't reach from his or her normal stance. If the batsman moves to bring the ball within reach, it won't be called a wide.

Glossary

Appeal   A shout of 'How's that?' to the umpire by one or more fielders, asking for a batsman to be given out.

Backing up (batting)   The non-striker starting to walk down the pitch as the ball is bowled, in case there's a chance of a quick run.

Backing up (fielding)   One fielder covering a team-mate in case of a mistake.

Bouncer   A fast, short-pitched delivery that reaches the batsman at shoulder height or higher.

Declaration   The voluntary close of its innings by the batting side even though all ten wickets have not been lost.

Duck   A batting score of nought.

Extras   Any runs that result from no-balls, byes, leg byes and wides.

Leg bye   A run from a ball that has come off some part of the batsman's body other than the hand.

Maiden   An over in which no runs are scored.

Off side   The side of the field in front of the batsman standing sideways at the crease.

On side   The side of the field behind the batsman standing sideways at the crease.

Overthrow   A fielder's return that eludes the wicketkeeper so that the batsmen are able to take extra runs.

Padding up   When a batsman plays no stroke to a ball and allows it to hit his or her pads. The batsmen cannot run leg byes when this occurs.

Tailender   One of the last batsmen in the batting line-up.

Taking guard   When a batsman asks the umpire to direct his or her bat in line with middle, middle and leg, or leg stump.

Walking   The action of sporting batsmen who, knowing that they have snicked a catch, immediately start walking off the field before waiting to see if the umpire gives them out.

Yorker   A ball that pitches around the batsman's feet. A straight yorker is one of the best wicket-taking balls.

Further information

Useful addresses

Australian Cricket Board
90 Jolimont Street
Jolimont
Victoria 3002
Australia

Board of Control for Cricket
in India
Chinnaswamy Stadium
Mahatma Gandhi Road
Bangalore 560 001
India

Board of Control for Cricket
in Pakistan
Gaddafi Stadium
Lahore
Pakistan

Board of Control for Cricket
in Sri Lanka
35 Maitland Place
Colombo 7
Sri Lanka

British Association for
Cricketers with Disabilities
Wisholme
St Martins Road
Gobewen
Oswestry
Shropshire SY11 3PL
England

National Cricket Association
Lord's Cricket Ground
London NW8 8QN
England

New Zealand Cricket
Council
PO Box 958
109 Cambridge Terrace
Christchurch
New Zealand

United Cricket Board of
South Africa
PO Box 55009
Northlands 2116
South Africa

Women's Cricket
Association
Yorkshire Cricket School
41 St Michael's Lane
Headingley
Leeds LS6 3BR
England

Further reading

The Art of Captaincy by Mike Brearley (Coronet, 1986)

Batting Made Easy by Stuart Moore (ICC Press, 1990)

Get Ready For Cricket by Stuart Biddle, Peter Morris, Anne De Looy and Peter Thomas
(Crowood Press, 1991)

Line and Length – A Bowler's Guide by Nick Ames (Charles and Roope Associated Press, 1989)

The Skills of Cricket by Keith Andrew (Crowood Press, 1984)

Index   Numbers in **bold** refer to captions.

Ambrose, Curtley **21**
Ashes, the 7
Australia 6, 7, 9
Azharuddin, Mohammed 12, **17**

back defence shot 17-18
bats 43
batting 12-20
  backlift 14
  follow-through 22, 23
  grip 13
  stance 13-14
batting gloves 44
'bodyline' series 6
Boon, David **15**
Border, Allan **14**
Botham, Ian 9, 12, **34**
bowling 21-5
  delivery of the ball 22
  fast bowling 23, 33
  grip of the ball 22
  run-up 22
  spin bowling 24-5, 33
  swing bowling 23-4, 33
Brittin, Jan **15**
byes 10

captaincy 32
  and batting 33-4
  and fielding 33
catching 31
Chamberlain, Jo **22**
clothing 44
Crowe, Martin **19**

drive shots 15-16

England 6, 7, 9, 32
equipment 43

fielding 10, 29-31
  defensive interception 30
  one-handed interception 29-30
fitness 35-8
forcing shot 19-20

forward defence shot 14-15

Gatting, Mike **35**
Gooch, Graham **13**, **38**
Gower, David **31**, 37
Grace, W.G. 7

helmets 44
Hick, Graham **28**
history and development of cricket
  6-9

ICC 6
India 6, 9, **35**

Khan, Imran **8**, 9, **16**

Lamb, Allan **43**
lbw law 39, 45
leg byes 10
Lewis, Chris **40**
line and length 21, 41
Lord's 6, 7

MCC 6
McDermott, Craig **29**
Melbourne 6
Miandad, Javed **26**
More, Keiran **28**

net practice 12, 39, 40
New Zealand 7, 9
no-balls 10, 11, 45

Packer, Kerry 7
pads 43-4
Pakistan 8, 9
pull shot 17

Richards, Viv **4**, 9, 12
Richardson, Richie 18, **33**
rules of the game 45
running between the wickets 20

Smith, Robin **42**

South Africa 9
square cut 18-19
Sri Lanka 9
Stewart, Alec **26**
sweep shot 16

Warne, Shane 25
West Indies **5**, 6, 7, 9
wicketkeeping 26-8
  stance 26
wides 10, 11, 45
women's cricket 7

Younis, Waqar 23